POLYVERSE

BOOKS BY LEE ANN BROWN

Cultivate (Tender Buttons, 1991)

Crush (Leave Books, 1993)

poems by Lee Ann Brown (We Press, 1993)

*a **muse**me* (Boog Literature, 1993)

Miss Traduction: Translations & Collaborations
(Tender Buttons, 1995)

The Voluptuary Lion Poems of Spring
(Tender Buttons, 1997)

Polyverse (Sun & Moon Press, 1999)

Lee Ann Brown

Polyverse

NEW **A**MERICAN **P**OETRY
SERIES · **31**

SUN & MOON PRESS
LOS ANGELES · 1999

Sun & Moon Press
A Program of The Contemporary Arts Educational Project, Inc.
a nonprofit corporation
6026 Wilshire Boulevard, Los Angeles, California 90036

This edition first published in paperback in 1999 by Sun & Moon Press
10 9 8 7 6 5 4 3 2 1
FIRST EDITION
©1999 by Lee Ann Brown
Biographical material ©1999 by Sun & Moon Press

This book was made possible, in part, through contributions to
The Contemporary Arts Educational Project, Inc.,
a nonprofit corporation

Some of these poems were previously published in the magazines and anthologies
*A.bacus, Aerial, Archeus, Astarte, Black Bread, Black Mountain II Review, Brief, The Broadside, Cathay,
Capilano Review, Clerestory, Cold Water Broadside, cuz, Epoch, Fire Readings:
A Collection of Contemporary Writing from the Shakespeare & Co. Benefit Readings, Front,
Hamilton College Anthology, Hyena, The Imperceptient, Interruptions, lingo, Ma!,
New York Magazine, O-blek: Writing from the New Coast, Out of This World: An Anthology of
the St. Mark's Poetry Project, The Poetry Project Newsletter, Pome, Raddle Moon,
Primary Trouble: An Anthology of Contemporary American Poetry, Red Weather, Rift, Score, 6ix,
The Shambhala Sun, Shiny International, Southern Poetry Review, Southerners, Talisman,
Tender Broadsides, Thermos/Thelma 5, 13th Moon, Torque, Trembling Ladders, Trouble,
We Magazine,*and *The World.* Some of these poems also appeared in the recordings "The of a The,"
music by Sarah Boyd Blair, *State of the Union* (zOaR Music); "Pledge," music by Elliott Sharp,
Beneath the Valley of the Ultra Yahoos (zOaR Music); and "Tech Pledge,"
music by Elliott Sharp and Carbon, *Lip:* A collection of spoken word artists to benefit
the Women's Action Coalition (Ruby Throat).
Some of these poems originally appeared in *Cultivate, poems by Lee Ann Brown, Crush* and *a **muse**me.*
The author would like to thank the editors and publishers of these works. She would also like
to express gratitude for support through a fellowship from the New York Foundation for the Arts,
The Fund for Poetry, and from residencies at the MacDowell Colony
and the Djerassi Resident Artists Program.

Cover: Elizabeth Murray, *Children Meeting*, 1978
©1997, Whitney Museum of American Art, New York
Purchased with funds from the Louis and Bessie Adler Foundation, Inc.,
Seymour M. Klein, President
Photograph ©1988 by Steven Sloman, New York
Design: Katie Messborn
Typography: Guy Bennett

LIBRARY OF CONGRESS CATALOGING IN PUBLICATION DATA
Brown, Lee Ann [1963]
Polyverse
p. cm _ (New American Poetry: 31)
ISBN: 1-55713-290-9
I. Title. II. Series.
811'.54_dc20

Printed in the United States of America on acid-free paper.

For Bernadette Mayer

Contents

Her Hearsay Hymnbook

Comfit   21

Witch Alphabet   33

Velocity City

A Little Resistance

There is a Zone whose even Years
No Solstice interrupt—
　　　—EMILY DICKINSON

Any letter is an alphabet.
When this you see you will kiss me.
　　　—GERTRUDE STEIN

Her Hearsay Hymnbook

People do gossip
—SAPPHO

Come go with me out to the Field —
To look upon the Rose
Whose glow — remembers once the Sun
Gave Garnets for her Clothes

Her crimson Cadence soon will Stop —
The music of the Spheres
Won't cease — but barely register
A Fraction of Earth's years

While Light still vibrates on our Brow
The subtle Minutes drag —
The Fly is droning with the Bee —
Our outer Bodies flag

18   There is a Zoochore whose even Yeasayers
      No Solute interrupt—
      Whose Sunbow constructs perpetual Nootka Cypress,
      Whose perfect Sea Squirts wait—

      Whose Summer Squash set in Summer Squash, till
      The Cephalic Indices of Jungle Gymns
      And Cephalic Indices of Auld Lang Syne fuse
      And Consensus—is Nootka Cypress.

The of a The

Alphabet uniforms steadily assault abroad —
A water power to any other plush.
The child element flowers —
and each pain makes a torture Zone.

Beds never can contain words
Whose ample deathless axis stands
At June — and each color
Has my one blank snow to bed.

I would read her an invisible genesis —
A rack the many syllables define —
No me is there —
Well as anybody is
If ecstasy was —

This comes of whose period
Can make the sentences soon.

Comfit

Words

weren't enough for her.

She often made
high cat cries
and danced hard
on the blue carpet.

list for summer

read books backwards
make love with a woman
lick wet leaves if thirsty
remind paper clips of the future
keep seaweed handy for snacks
collect words on scraps of paper
knit some voodoo stockings with that hair I've been
                                        saving

After Sappho

24   So many people
advised me against you.
How glad I am
we could not resist.

White Slippers

When I reach for the lamp,
my thumb goes into
the bowl of water by my bed.

Even the book just bought
is missing, as my shoes
are heading for the door.

Cafeteria

Ice Tea
Cream corn
Fried okra
plus one meat

El Floridita

BW & 177th
grilled chicken
cassava
drink ($2)
"to die dreaming"
orange

The A

Young
Black
Exec

Books
on
his lap:

How to Get on the Fast Track

Nods
Exhausted

Somewhere around 125th

Chain reaction

When one guy
smokes, seems like
they all do.

Subway Exchange

What time is it?
   A little after nine.
At night, right?

Tender skin under the edge of your shirt.

You sing "beauty"
while hair falls across her
painful face.

I sit here breathing.

Miss
Inexactitude

28   tulip skirt

                trade off to point blank
affect
             sugar and tree camera

               will you
          bottle this stuff

both

both my lovers are broke
3 broke lovers
all my loves are broke

Crawling into bed
        away from
        the crowd

When will
    someone come
        looking for me?

At the cluttered table

waiting for no one in particular

I suddenly remember

your turning towards me

Long hair
Black clothes
Hoop earrings

Netsuke

Brochure

A reading
folded into sections
free tamper
logic jumps logic

Oshinko

I sit too close
to the couple talking

This learning
to be alone
goes on & on
like rain represented
by straight black lines

beads

sleep   pressed   disk
   kiss   sac   curl
lint   tendon   nag
  gowned   do   oral
lapidary   ypsilanti
 ismaili   ike   ebb

Witch Alphabet

```
Z  Y  X
   W  V
U  T  S
R  Q  P
O  N  M
L  K  J  I
H  G  F  E
D  C  B  A
```

Mayakovsky

You too, Meow Aooo, cactus flower
deepening little river
chant beat on my back, a veil of hair!
Arch fish–
Rabbit-like strokes, carnivorous
animal eyes, your nipples at dusk!

Arch
3 times, but numbers collide–
even vowels tend to dissolve,
rubbing all I am:
(untranslatable)

Catweight!

Pledge

I pledge allergy to the flail of the United States of
      Amigo.
And to the reputation for which it stands,
      one national park, under godmother, indivisible,
with lice and kabob for allegiance.

I pledge allegory to the flagellant of the United Statistic
      of Ammunition.
And to the reproduction for which it stands, one
      naughtiness, under good, indivisible,
with lick and juvenile for anatomy.

I pledge allelomorph to the flagelliform of the United
      State-of-the-Art of American English.
And to the repudiation for which it stands, one nation-
      alism, under go-getter, indivisible,
with library science and juvenile court for Alleluia.

On my hop, I will try
to serve godmother, my coup de grâce,
and to live by the give-and-take scramble lawn

On my hoodlum, I will try
to serve goose, my coupon,
and to live by the gladioli scrap heap laxative.

On my honors of war, I will try
to serve go-go dance, my country music,
and to live by the gizmo scowl lawyer.

Love

38   Love of manifestos motion slow,
heavenly like smell will. We
cock and you suck. I'll breasts
my squeeze if event cultural favorite.

"My O cute she's," say you when agree I.
Girls past at grin; you, me and you said "you."
Time   one   watch. Your is bed to wear you thing.
Only the lap your onto leap, flying a take to want I love.

ii

I want the only thing: one   you   when,
"O squeeze your cock like heavenly slow
to take you time," you said. "Grin," you say,
"My, my, breasts," and we motion.

A flying wear-to-bed at past, she's favorite.
Leap onto you is you and me girls, cute cultural.
I'll will manifestos, lap your watch.
I agree event if you suck and smell of love.

iii

I want to take a flying leap onto your lap.
The only thing you wear to bed is your watch.
One time you said, "You and me."
You grin at past girls. I agree

when you say, "She's cute."
O my favorite cultural event, if you
squeeze my breasts, I'll suck your cock and we
will smell like heavenly slow motion manifestos of love.

Gossip North Carolina

40   She makes up the bed
from the "backside of the desert,"

Telling me the how of things:
"A woman's tongue is like unto a serpent's tooth,"
saying
                "Heresy! Heresy!"

and me thinking
she's saying
Atlantic Ocean — "Terror Sea"

I mark vines in the morning

Come back
Find them grown over the road

Prunes

for C.D. Wright

Gloves wilt like lilies in the woman's bedside drawer.
Every night she creams her hands with vaseline

And wears them to protect the sheets. Her husband sleeps
in the next room except on weekends. She snores

and wakes at four in the morning to wash his fine hair.
Breakfast ready. Scuppernongs pop like tadpoles

into a snake's mouth. Those prunes are good for you
and mean plums in French she says as he nods at the sun.

The Day the War Started

42   My cat catches a baby mouse.
I take birth control pill number three.
Kim says a cloud in the shape of a cross was spotted
      over Washington D.C. and that Barbara Bush's broken
      leg is a sign.

I go to the Russian baths.
A woman washes me.
Someone has written on her steamy mirror:
      "Visualize Peace."
I go upstairs to have Borscht.
The television says:
The War Has Officially Begun
Numerous very large explosions
The first weapons are Tomahawks
A million dollars apiece

This according to Ed Peck
and Gary Sick.
As we speak
Before our eyes.

Those with the Pointed Hats Consult
Secretly with my Mother in the Corner

Home is the sweet pill I take every night
My mother turns it slowly over in her once soapy palm
Like a hard communion wife

Home is the fluorescent light drawer
Packed horribly with meaning
Dead peoples' phone numbers
New clothes don't skip it

Home is where I discover many small bruises dancing
In front of the mirror to *How Sweet it is to be Loved by You*
Home is I don't know where my stuff is
Home has more leaves in front than when I lifted off

> *It's like Jelly, baby*

> She so seldom sleeps
> A cool chance
> You should rest
> But not that much

> Unmanageable allergies
> Stoned in love
> Violet   Green   Blue

Yale Place

44   Play ash cat
and your sister is other,
she's not the only other
you have no brother.
Your father is slow and wonderful mother is a root.
We watch TV
and eat meat.
The witch show comes on,
Dark Shadows mother won't allow.
The sandbox hides
the metal kettle. Sister kicks
Pears for butter. Teah's tire swing.
William has a school to attend immediately.
We boil marbles to make angels.
He picks up a rock for the salamander
and builds a three-story tree house.
Pirates.
Dan has a professional tree house and holds "Crate Myrtle."
Years later William grows bonsai,
I paint a slug with a magenta background
in Freedom Park, now lost in a museum.
The tangled conjunction of fences. Suck on Mimi's hair.
Puppet stage I hide behind not to go to the crowded bathroom.
Mommy has a zebra.
Dad has nipples.
The squareback is a lemon.
Papier-maché puppet party. Violets in the sideyard.
Mr. & Mrs. O.'s little paths, recorded trains.

Park mecca must wait till the day-old bread.
She falls on a mat of spines.
The Dr.'s Batman glasses magnify his eyes.

It snows on mother's earrings.
She immediately melts them with her lipstick.
Through a crack a strange man watches TV.
Little match girl by the steam iron.
Jiffy pop and revealed snow.

Box turtle returned to the stream
on speeding night, father bikes in back.
Kneel to cry this is how.

Paper dolls we're moving in. Janie thinks they're worms.
Cement bridge over a hole. Mrs. Sting Wray.
I come home from being Dutch to find my mother Chinese.
We cook in the paper.

Sister washes the turtles with soap.
Uh-piss-cuh-bull Church.
Extracted raisin on Thanksgiving day.

Eat a whole peeled apple in bed with Winnie-the-Pooh
        spinning.
Disney rituals, later resulting in
late night
turnip white
orb eating to sleep.

She Sings to the Little Animals
on Her Bed

They are Sailor Boy, Little Ballerina and Poppy-Pops.
The Glow-in-the-Dark Man comes into her room.
The red radio tower blinks on by the far-off train noise.
The ceiling fan opens cool slats through to the attic.
She can smell the ghostly curtains.

I look out my window and see a door into the light,
          so I run and jump through it.
I run around the house three times in my underwear.
The bed falls down.

I get her to drink the beauty potion
          made of marshmallows and french dressing.

I am stranded on a tiny beach against a cliff
          while monster sharks and whales
          with huge, pointy teeth roil up out of the water.
It's too crowded for them to even swim,
          and they're getting madder.
I wake up holding Raggedy Ann's leg as a rope.
My parents are looking down at me from the headboard.

We hold a parade against trash and go to the stream to clear it
          out after church.

The Borrowers move into my bookcase.
We build tepees out of bamboo and blankets in the back yard.

I do magic by lighting a candle in a shallow bowl of water.
When I put the glass over it, the candle goes out
and the water gets sucked up into the glass vacuum.

She shows me the place in the church nursery closet
        where the escaped slave tunnel was sealed up
        after the cave-in.

We sit in the bottom of another closet to start the Pink
    Panther club.
The first item on the agenda is to name our new cat
        after one of his body parts.

And then she sings:

And little Sailor Boys
and Little Ships
and Little Indians
all the way,
all the way,
with all the way.

And little flowers,
and little flowers,
and little babies like loo,
and little babies like loo.

Point Blue

A woman eating alone requires no explanation. My response to their ad was never answered. Teal highlighted with a bittersweet orange. All of my friends were embarrassed by the price. I push the button and all of the fire doors close. Silver ladles hang in front of a red canister, swinging slightly. I leave the building as the engines pull up in the rain. Tip preferred in cash. On the jukebox: *Morning Has Broken* by Cat Stevens, *Cry for Love* by Iggy Pop, *Barracuda* by Heart, *Loosey's Rap* by Rick James, *God Bless the Child* by Billie, and *Beep a Freak* by I forget who. Pretty girl station. What's your destination? Oh, any old thing. So get to work. Deva gives me the Chills. She says,
I need a bare neck.
Concentrate on what I'm saying.
Concentrate on what I'm saying.
Babies are crying. People are dying.
Concentrate on what I'm saying.
Crack an egg on your head and let the yolk drip down,
        the yolk drip down, the yolk drip down.
Concentrate. Concentrate.
Stab a knife in your back and let the blood drip down,
        the blood drip down, the blood drip down.
Criss Cross Applesauce.
Spiders are crawling up your back.
Spiders are crawling down your back.
Spiders are crawling all around.

Tight squeeze.
Cool breeze.
Now you've got the,
got the,
got the CHILLS.

Coffee

50   Put the coffee on and keep going.
She is liking the one took money right out of her
purse. There lies the tunnel
miles under the hill.

Give me civil rights
or uncivil things will start to happen.
I'm only a bitch anyhow.

Throw up my hands and go home.
That silly man wrote pens prick the page.
The little bear writes her pins prick my skin.
She marks me down.
She marks me well.
Grammar changing daily.

Even as we speak I might be writing
an acrostic with your name.
What's the use
in cutting up? What about explosives?
I glow among poets.
Dress up for it. Unspeakable.

Sweet. Condensed milk in Vietnamese Coffees.
Platanos in sour cream at Mary's
where she mistook me for the Virgin.
Sex which was fluent in all tongues on and off the streets

of Inner Mission.
Free Patsy from the jukebox: Yes
it turned me on, it might turn on me. Violet
air too picaresque to be caught. Voluptuous

Landscape rushing past. Who am I
without her? I feel
I'll find out soon enough. Mean
while I'm in pleasurable danger
of staying up all night. Further riots.

Spilling scarves, plants, light, gesticulate
with my eyes.   Page, do you know of words
using Y as a vowel? Try. By Monday. Man
you script my permission slip. An under
garment silky slipping back

into my top drawer alongside
laid aside toys. Djuna.
Dear jewel, have you come
across the rush roof that catches
desert wind, making it cooler?

(Rustling of language underneath.)
Are you landed yet? Do you work among people
speaking? Working and speaking you are among them.
In the speaking are you writing? I write
to you amidst the writing. Still think of you

despite the living. Around us are so many tongues.
The vast universal dictionary. The vowels.

A voice will counterpoint to question. I know you.
A sign here at school says "Rescue the referent." Fall

River for a drink? Light in the eyes.
Desert song, the trucks were throwing past us.
We stopped for nothing. Blood on our hands,
under nails as we stopped at the gas oasis.

Save grapes for water. Hat Book Paper
Every noun becomes a verb. Play Check Travel
Every verb a noun. I want to punch you out.
I'm walking television. I'm a mess. Do what you want.
Coffee's expensive, wish it would go down. Redaction.
Leather jacket stolen despite the hole. A wild thing

with language is what I deserve. Desire the way she's
less referential. The night
you called the dream was about you two.
At the pool moving the same way.
Hiding, your mother caught me in a towel, forgave me.

But this was a dream.
Theo thinks Utopias are fascistic, too
perfect, a monumental bore.
Preserve pre-verse perverse.
But then we'll never spit it out:
"Be a man."

Performance tonight: 7 O'clock.
We'll all live together until then.
All the saints:

Maria, Theresa,
Joan, Cecelia,
Bernadette, Gwen, Claire,
Agnes,
Mater Dolorosa,
Oh Mary don't you weep.

Dora Dunlop Woolfolk Draper —
She liked elk meat best. Stitched silk
over her hymn book approved by the Holy Fathers.
Wrote in back: "Women either Love or Hate."

Journey of my soul. Got yanked back to the ranch
from schooled elucidation because she wanted to be
a nun. Slept in a piano box. Met Indians.

No saints in the South, only tar and greens. Food
for the soul. Protestants don't even protest. One word
sentences from Louisiana jails: Kool. Mute. OK. Inked.
Aunt Cordelia who met Thomas Wolfe and now collects
"beach relics." Vowel sounds stacked in racks, living

color. "Enjoiee" "Feathuh." Breathe your "ʀ's" away,
add extra syllables in the vowels. The history of Lee
doesn't interest me except etymologically right now.
Sum it up: The sense of place is not where I'm wanting.

Oracular history. A kiss. Carolina shout. Fifty dollar
paycheck. The earth is narrow and the fullness thereof,
them and those that dwell therein.

The Thousand-and-One Nights
of the Inside-Out Gown

She's a minor flirt,
              a cloud in trousers.
Contractual diseases,
              waking up every hour.

Lifting belly, pivoting
the horoscope to her advantage.

Today: three women as they say
while at the sink sucking on oysters
appear as altarpieces, minor miracles
in triptych. Screwdrivers, pliers, tobacco
flirt with the fabled dioxin molecule.

M-space and x-height poised on a step-stool.
Ruby carrots (cooked with butter and white sugar.)
Ruby cabbage: with bacon grease and lots of pepper.
Serve with 15,000 Meows.

Graffiti Arrest. The voice
over is in a male whisper.
Put in some moon and lilies.

If you vamp out I'll stake you without even thinking about it.

Obaa made me some Sally Lunn: a heavenly sweet
yellow leavened bread. Actually indescribable.
I'm so amazed I can writing.

The Rake is revived
as they're all breaking quickly:
Bee By Design,
Crisco King,
Speedo Elvis,
Bishop Rambo,
Ms. Pronounce
and Fabled Dennis
and it's Rose's Pepito on the inside track.

Blue water verses stasis.
The shapeless morning suddenly writes a beautiful hand.

Dreams Listing

1

A small purple bird is on its androgynous animal shelf. I ask it to step out onto my wet finger. It does and turns into a tiny man dressed in a grey suit. Everything becomes a shiny white page with flat black type, floating up and away.

2

In an elevator, a bear lies on a stretcher wrapped in white bandages, a puzzled hurt face. Gorillas in a zoo, decaying society. Men's heads have been found outside their cages. Having no money makes you appreciate what's public and free — stonework and architecture.

3

Entering the cubicle, I find submersed in a tank of warm water — half calf, half child, in tans and blues. I go get Louise to prove it's real.

4

Dancing with a shark as Phoebe Cates. In church, the balcony railings are wooden, intricately carved as the choir sings. We're late.

5

I bear a huge sensitive penis, erect past my waist. Anne is around, a little doll of herself in hand complete with outfit. She is socializing with restauranteers in Charlotte.

I'm giving a poetry reading at 12:30 at night. Everyone will be tired.

6

India and a bunch of girls make a line, dancing naked in the grass. I want to film them but the Super-8 isn't working.

7

I say to Mom something that implies I'm sleeping with Jones Doughton, the towhead who used to chase girls in Sunday school. At the Ear Inn this unknown poet Maureen Owen brought in from the country is reading. I'm distracted and offer to get 2 addresses for him: "Liz" or "Zil".

8

My father is driving me and the family in the car. A snake and a friendly rat live in the floorboards. A color print poster of the snake is to be made for the play.

Thang

after Ginsberg & Mayer

58   With a milkweed pod

With a white cat on your lap on your minister's bed
where you later touch your first girlfriend's nipple and
start to cry

In the car in front of your parents house while you're
home for a visit with a boy from high school surprised at
how nice it feels

Up against the car on the side of the highway in the
middle of the Mojave desert with huge semis going by
One of you has your period.

In a Japanese treehouse in a youth hostel near Brunswick
Georgia with j & j after drinking rum josh leaves julie
and I stay on & on

In half dream with the guy who brings the lunch

With poets you read

On your side or back with him coming up behind you
from the side, you thrust downwards

Being on top pressing down with your bone on his or her
thigh or pelvic bone your fingers in her or on you if you
are a man and or a woman

Or this way with your fingers in me from the back your
arms are long enough

Slowly licking your cunt or cock, your cock going inside
and outside my mouth you never know which

Worrying and sucking and circling your clit, tasting your
cunt while at the same time you're pulling fingers in and
out of you only after kissing down your neck very slowly to
get there

In memory that doesn't make you sad or anticipatory

With a purple dildo borrowed from Patty

In the middle of the day even though we have visitors in
the next room

Under the new paper umbrella I just bought in Japantown.
We miss the dance.

On the Murphy bed which makes lots of noise

On your back I touch you and come you make me stop.

In the piano room on the floor I'm in my tennis shoes and
Sarah's pink gown saying "I'm ready" later, "Better get it!"

Right after your tour twice to the same Beatles album
while my guitar gently weeps

In the hottub place in downtown SF because we were
living at your parents'

At the Columns in New Orleans after that dream of
wearing wet silk joined onto your dream of the shining
ocean, hot though for the air conditioner, it's dark when
we wake up moving then we go out to eat soul food or
crawdad jambalaya several times

On acid and you think he's a horse you & I go up and
up and both feel it but you're all over him the next day
and the next year

We're in the front seat they're in the back I didn't like
when you stood up and pissed by the creek after
turning around when we were only kissing sticking your
cock in my throat and coming uninvited so I straighten
my foot in my character shoes and crack your mother's
windshield that was not a way of making love

In the treehouse where I played Narnia and lost my
purple sweater with pearl buttons we rub together with
our clothes on

By the pool I put you in my mouth you come out
before you come you're scared of me

I hold you down and press

I bring you Krispy Kremes after church you're still in
bed and stretch up out of the blankets

You suck on my nipples for what seems like three hours
as the 8-track of Cat Stevens goes around and around

You let me touch you after months and months you
taste like lobster bisque and honey

In the press to the coatroom after the Rosewood Ball
you put your fingers in my cunt while I look over your
shoulder I don't need your name

On the floor in the empty room you are amazed I've ( )
but haven't fucked yet

Occasionally Named

I'm awed and we laugh with questions, artless
Of me to speak so ungenerally of thee & thy name
— BERNADETTE MAYER
from "Sonnet"

poem for lisa

the card return trip outré spicer dictttation
i'm not worthy i dont feel the martians
i supplicate the tender feet of younger
attic no sapphic islands which we are too
old ironically to be on we cant be younger
than sappho's girls a new language justifies
my love the old tools what can we do is
play still a ploy I like your new one way
every other street you're too old too dont fit
the generation thank you transhistorical you
are building a building of fairest notprose
something new but totally knowing and even

loving the older "beat" keeps coming why
is the amazing spacing different keeping going

Demi-Queer Notion

66   As I pinch my nipples & think of you
I'm sorry Frank O'Hara isn't as cute
          as you expected
Let's go to the beach and process
all of the ways I looked up
and saw you walking on a
snowy field against blue sky
in your cute tight genes
blue   Everyone adores you
including me Let's go
to lunch at Frimps
and eat french Liz food on
a silver palate complete with
difficult obscure obdurate
obfuscation or brilliant
men men men why the fuck can
I not get into reverse ever
of course they'll be chivalrous (ever) &
you, driver of radio stick
not caring drink a beer in the fifties
modernistic or max fish post
no future? I don't think so

To Jennifer M.,

while drinking in the GCB

Let's make out in the girl's room!
Let me write you a wild heart
        with my favorite flowerdy pen—
But it couldn't surpass yours
beating so multiaviariously
in your left aligned margin.

What's with these people
boys or girls who tamp down
the lyric impulse, the heart
waiting in line, barefoot &
illegal. Old-fashioned emotion
is relegated to a loud radio
void sometimes, but Frank O'Hara
has faith in you & me even
though or because we're girls.

My Evans

68   The other is always there if ever we
live apart from each other which
we damn well might considering
the exigencies of academic & non working
conditions spread fearfully across the
awful MLA plains of Midwest Wasteland but
this is depressing we can always be mail devotees if
we're not too busy I think I'll always remember your
wearing the bells of Beckettish Sazerac Star Twins Hello Kitty
Continuum & how one "Steven of Providence"
sang 70's songs with me at Lisa's
rubbing my nose upwards and around
forbidden sexy to other boys but find
a place for you ever in my heart
I'm already on line 13 and haven't
       even yet begun to THANK YOU
sonnetly for being and yourself & my
believer I believe we will find
many new late night thoughts and
dinners in this now still abundant
divine Providence we are fortunate
enough to bear resemblance to & despite & because of
knowing how long your cock is friends
boomerang where poetry is

Poem for Joe

written around Joe Brainard's 50th birthday

I've always wanted to write you a poem
      So here it is!

I loved watching your eyes tonight
      when you read your poems
      for Jimmy Schuyler
I love the way you walk
      your long legs and arms swinging
      blue cashmere fast off into the
      cold night after pouring me wine
I love your whippet pictures
      your Pansies & Nancy
      All your flowers . . .
  and the line drawings of boys in
      underwear
          with that little bulge
or their cocks actually out
               arching over the thigh
        like the one in Allen's bathroom
I love when you brought me
         Campari & soda with lemon
      down by the lake
        and extra lemon to make my hair
            blonder
    last summer
      or was it the summer before
I love floating on rafts quietly

        like water bugs
     trying not to get too wet
       in the sun
I love your style
I love your interview in Little Caesar Magazine
I love "I Remember"
     and that you're from Oklahoma

I love the shape of your head (a fine skull)
          and that you got some white shirts
    at New Republic

I love your soft kiss
    goodbye or hello

Taxi
Thank You

Ulysses Flaubert
Azhar Islam
Robert Quach
Faisel Ahmed
Angel Rodriguez
Samu Nematella
Lulzim Borova
Edgar Santana
Gabriel Leander
Michele Robinson
Jean Cadet
Carlos Camargo
Antonio Rodriguez
Jose Batista
Mian Saled
Gurpreet Singh
Simon Ng
Ahmed Ahmed
Herman Herbst
Sergio Burgos
Mohsin Chaudry
Emmanuel Sable

August Valentine

72 Asymptotic rays play her changes—
Anne's necking with her best breaths
Beneath and/or above our ears where
Treeish thoughts twine as vibrantly as DNA.

Lushly oval or orally ornate
accidents keep pace in spheric musics. Her timing
divines Steinian, while white, green, red, blue Taraesque
buzzing liquids camp out on an eastern slope.
The surprise comes continually in
pink weather. Her six seasons consist

of Upper Thaw, Rose Mist, Stirring Panther,
Bee Bomber, Spaced Rain and Cobalt Song.
Transmission loves a vessel or letter,
unseemly, pushed through the slot—so
your poems fetch my pleasure as I
embed your name via a spread room. You
travel such a continental divide.

Sestina Aylene

Beginning to pen a verse
I think of you–
what you must love
to do and do with ease:
Present a fruit or number
As from an empty

drawer. What's as empty
as the way we begin? Averse
to all Eve's droppers who number
our ways? Fact is, you
do much to ease
the why of Miss P. Love

or Funk: letter out. Love
letters love to be read as empty
poems or flowers named ❤'s ease,
the way a verse
faces to or on or in you,
for you can only then begin to number,

never delimiting that number
of ways in which you love
to make a poem. You
can tell a story of empty
necessity, a ring averse
to being filled too easily, to ease

simple closure. Easy
readings are possible but soon outnumber
even each other. A verse
demands a second love,
a torn page. Empty
breath slows through it, you

are surprised, you
read it slowly over, ease
into its second skin. Empty
fruits multiply and renumber
spaces to fill out love,
for ways to make a verse

not averse to being held a little longer. You
love to run and ease
into numbers of empty stays or stars.

74

A Present Beau Epithalamion

for Stacy Doris & Chet Weiner

New Northwest seas win a 75
        toast by Torah's code.
The search of when, what, why, and who twine
        to these wedded threads' consent.

A Corona on them!
        In this said tryst, ecstasy chases!
Inner irises arise!
        Tread the hewn air!
Raid and redress addicted chinaware!
Dish oasis rodeo odes!
        Retain net snow!

Io's Roster:
        Attendants to the wedded two:
Isis and Osiris
        of Ohio and Rio
(Switch hitters as new acts),
        Wrens, Cats, Hares, Swans, Toads and Rhinos–
Circe's sows wrest the door away to go too–
        It's a sin not to attend this do!

The Sirens act tender, ridden
        'tween the coast and star
Drawn, redrawn and dressed
        in stately, restated earth,
Earth's son's hint indented her north by northwest.

She stinted and said, "Aye."

No AIDS, warts, witches, windy Cindys
        nor chinchie tittie rats
Dare send hindrance
        nor drat this tract.

You TNT renters wade in strewn ways,
        Stay tenderly tented in dense heat.

Arid or wetter,
        the way a wine
or name
        becomes an intense one.

A best behest
        in you says:

                Do it now.
                Do it newer.

Gerard for Unction

waking up late and messy
appear in the again Adonais
one more line than a sonnet
our textured desk fresh between
crushing trucks in true source park
not too much grammar worldly
jaggerish tonka birds spill
a very white sneaker what
comes into your head cruise
across addressed to the same
where was thy mighty mother
when you lay thinking out late knees
not Adonais or ironic spectacular print you're
the mother and younger sister of me rustled up

Present Beau
Robin Blaser

Able laser seer in rose
        An eros orb or ball
        Rare, rare lobelia rails
        A noble nib
        Robed and born

*a **muse**me*

"By 'museme' he means 'the basic unit of musical expression which in the framework of one given musical system is not further divisible without destruction of meaning . . .'"

—*From me to you. Popular music as message,*
—RICHARD MIDDLETON

Clio Loco

O Oil Loci
I Loll, I Coo,
I Coil olio.

Lo, O ill ici,
Cool C.O.
Col. Clio

Apple Pie Epic

a lil' pill, Calliope

Clap ice, opal peace
OPEC oil papal lapel
OPP cloacal pee-pee á loo

A PC pet per clip laps
Los poco loco cops
Local police ape PLO pep

A pale caller leap
Capo a cola allele
Poplar calla lei, a loss
Pec elope, a polar cape

Erato, Aerator

A rear terror rate
or Rarer aorta art

Toro! Toro! Ta-Ra! A Rat!
Ratatattat to Tate

Era o' orator
To eat tree tar, 'tater tot or oreo torte:
Rote error:
Roto-Rooter Ratatrat R

Taro eater too
PTA Tao area or
A tea roarer otter
ate retro rot

Truer Pure Euterpe

84   Et tu, teuer Peter
Pert tree pet
Peer up yr. turret,
Utter tupperer

Tree turp erupt
Pret Purrrrr rep á P.R.
Eat up ept pu-pu,
Upper putterer

O No Melpomene

Re: Lone poem, pen nomme
Pommel pope poop
Olé, Olé, Ol' Pop Pomp

Pelé mope
Mono men pole, lop me
One pen open poem

Peel 'em:
La Pomme, pome, pommelo

Moon pone molé

Yoo-Hoo, Polyhymnia

86   A po' hymn hoopla
               in a Lollapaloolla Hall

I am Polly
Him: Nia
       a Nippon Mina Loy.

An alloy pony hool-a-hoop,
Amy lay in Hilton limp and 'nilla

Pomp Mon
Nepal
Hominy poi
Imp yo-yo all lampy
       in open hill hay

A Loopy Lap
An Oil Mop
A Pool Nope
A Pall in May

     Nay Pal,
     Pin yon piñon on yo' polo yoni

Holy Moly!
Monopoly Mania!

Pre-Terpsichorean Chores

hotter eros terror
core itch is cerise, rots prettiest,
sop, apest priss
piss shit this chore tipper
hic sop teaser sip
rise each peach photo

Posit tips
Tipi Sir: Tio Pepe is the hired Sire

pits it to tot psi später rape
chip seat teaches chit spore or
his sere heater hisses soap

pepper cherry sherry
terse, it tears, chirps

Thalia, Aha

88   A Hilt
      La Lait, ail hit

      Lila, Alta, Tia, Titia Lahti
              hit L.A. Hiat AA
      Hi All!

      Tall Thai hat
      A tilt halt lathe
      Lit tit an' tail it 'til Haiti

An Air

I, in Ainu rain
Unrun in Nara á Iran
Nur una Nana in Ur,
      an Ian in Narnia

Urania ran

Noon Eons

90   Yo, Mom, Mnemosyne
        née Nosy Synonym
        Yes?
        No?

        One sees neon syne
        Syn-
        Semo-

        Eno, Moe y Sons:
        Sony men
        No soy Mmes. . .

        O neo mneme!

CoLabs

Thought

I am sitting here right now with Lee Ann.
We wonder if Marie is asleep.
She is not, she is reading.
We are drinking beer.
We're wondering about what makes poetry.
We're wondering what each other is really thinking.
We hear the traffic, rushing water.
We go into separate rooms and back together again.
Yet we sit still not saying what we think of exigency,
      absolute value, Marie and of us as humans.
And still we don't write complex poems.
We let single words trigger streams of dialogue.
Marie turns the page in the next room.
Lee Ann remembers Bernadette talking about dream
      journeys and wants to go on one.
Bernadette is reading the Coltrane book.
It is a church that is devoted to I must say dreams
      or certain churchesthat have to do with eyedrops,
      ones that Mr. Coltrane himself here didn't know
      nothing about.
We will what?
We will go on singing you.

with Bernadette Mayer

Rakish Scrubbing of Graduate Gowns

94

Random senses down washed dishes
oh but no the dishes are unwashed
will you bend over in your gown
wash them I fuck you then
interested in workings counter to
how water touches the beep
of the machine already later
yesterday with Max is formal
& tomorrow with Sophia informal as if
the record is stuck, smoky plants
and feathers light fires down
right by the bears they look like her
& she might cross in the abstract fields
then while puzzling routes of tender
teas we rub shoulders of other each
& think then think we think & how
do people think women & men men &
          women think we think we want
to what? to puzzle shoulders to
          abstract it dash dash to
          be together—is it
          written right?
That that that means or is mean?
Playing, throwing, cheating gerunds
rolling drear carpets or folding buttons
at night
and as for participles yes this is
          how to begin again after all

& you will divest yourself of
           your silken woman's dress
or South Africa contrary I love you
silken syntax flung out the window
actually continuing unselfishly
nonreflexive nonprose sense
Every way a squirrel can jump
& how & why & why & why
I covet you against the commandment not to
I, like a squirrel jump at you at
           you no I can't say this—
ball's in your court don't cry
I'll give you time to jump start
we're overlapping now
I forgot that I ought
to say & then thou willst

to as a female be what?
Will you stay with me for a minute?

with Bernadette Mayer

i like the use of -emes like the way i want to eme you
like all of those Moxie filled women named Appliance
and fucksemes like the functuous fluxuous you of the
moment

Flexibly renting the twa corbies bedsteader
and fucksibly relenting the immanent gonad of twilight
and lovers and
women all named the same thing so as to forward
relations
and alternately different so as to foreground the
diaspora of usses
unroselike cohorts fret cracked and staffed—messed
out
likewise unpinked and strippen from the specificity of
morphemes
derivatively driven from the day diva blue water what
you wear as in the leopard, that i call natural and just as
much you
yours and ours ouch batten those rare churlish "we's"
and curlish fees like the we that forms from pearl and
pre pure
poor pubescent plaqueless ostensibly implacably pearly
puss
pussyesque oral jasmine jamming gemlike caliber tryst
christy
crystal and inklike image ally purely pungent and
picture penitence

or picture pentax not-less putrescence of
        pearlescent purls
Where are the usses older differ doing a line or
        that's it an
older purification of the do did done dog days
        or light years sung
or bright ears stung by a cunning linguist's
        sermonific sass
applied ripple nouge to thee and thy sepia sick
        not-theater
or thought thunken thistle to a plethorific past
        and proffered
nimbly as what lithe blithe and blissful prank
        disdains a plectral
crack plaza pitched where tinted shells dis-
        robed disrosed
rise to a polymorphous occasion and end dying
        fawning frugally.

with
Liz Fodaski & Ted Pearson

Immoblete

98   An informed choice, a lantern jaw, slatternly laws
                                pounce
announce   let him go then   ma please
instratification
A linked deck, anticipatory filth bridges
                         stratification
the freedom man   past tense   offen diffi
are you splitting the ger
                    und renounce jezt
jettage trommel pink or tinge lip
dont follow the differential maw upshit
kick it   on dem
(the woman is writing like an idiomatic)
more more more concepts appear(s) very
                         slowly
underlage promfit surcut adamantinemobile
(maw please   who is the idiot   you maw)
Slurp!   Bell cape
        flows a vowel inversion
        where alphabet city meets
        numbered collusion

maw the important part no you cant
say that yesm of this poem is that I'm
a white polar bear hear and er dusk
remember cant be seen after dusk maw

crazy beauty daily mixed too many eclipses
I'm open
the circus   circumstantial   immobility
high hit almost smothered or what
donedat scrat im sophistrail   draw
or claustrophobic sizzle I'm the ghost of
the James Brown of Ear Inn
going home   instate gufferama shucks

with Hannah Weiner

Two by Fours

100 Here we
Sit but
Where is
Our food?

More and
More means
Less than
Cowboy bar

Lee Ann
"Kiss me"
Euphemism maybe
we consolidate?

Diversifying rather
sparsely only
monkish chatter
at last

Let's go
surfin' now
scattered pines
wonder how

Glom Collom
through Brown
Jack Daw
Ora Lee

Carter Family
Not Jimmy
Peanutbutter yodels
Very baroque

Due wecognition
wuns down
my leg
weally fast

Squirrels rule
slim geometries
Inspire me
to longitude

Snow remains
up above
but now
12 flowers

Disjunctive bite
separates illusion
Cock cunt
Welsh landscape

with Jack Collom

Body in Trouble

Evocatively pull down thy hair
         to drown my cock in full softness
Sweet palmers at the mind
    find shin digs swirling fro discreet
       the largest organ skin
Far mesh these arms of ours begin

Nailing frames a windy binding
Kindness came to sing your thighs
Signing daughters of dubbed eyes
      of lids upon the plain of pancreas
Departmental lip extrusion
        concludes the shedding tongue

Mod joints tousle
bod points nestle
Corpus christy ankles
thankless gist fist muscle
is that mouth the mound
Or is it the round and learnéd arc of back?

with Jennifer Moxley

Master Beatty by Al Churinga

Not directly I was fucking
on my brothers all up to
far why wanted sidelines
combination of happening
entered blackmail young
toward my room for me
together on either side
older imagined noise out loud
hand over my imagining
state of how wrong even
to this day over me for
comes all over satisfied
larger family off with
just me and the boys more of
this thing not just poor families

with Jennifer Moxley

104 Stole   draped   remark
falls baby cajole a daylight flexible
western attic

        oh,   pleshette gather
comprehensive not fretting not hungry
not gentle not
gesturing vat valhalla   sappho
links right I
        might call against waffle

Sappho

fall a stole draped remark
oh baby, gather against
comprehensive gesturing not
        fretting, not waffle
not flexible daylight, I call might "western"
cajole hungry links, pleshette righter
valhalla vat
gentle attic

a baby daylight
pleshette falls fretting

cajole I stole
not not against

comprehensive waffle
attic links sappho

gentle hungry remark
draped falls, oh vat
righter gather

might not valhalla gesturing
flexible western

with Jennifer Moxley

Inner crawdad buzz

106   manic, a bout, twained and (sic)
standard Hiss tarts
kettle Juan Gris ottoman nestled hem.

A cue, says him of Nottingham.
Overt winged heifer "innie" buddy
get soft wren a seed bee comb
freesia bushes tit
too our hurls a tour,
Salmon on her bard's care
Hiawatha Romanoff Taliesin
kneads abutment honest code.

with Lisa Jarnot

A Double Triolet

Across the year each sentence goes
and turning falls to find its grace
unknowns of where the poem shows
across the years each sentence goes
the work is haunted by the whole
of moving plays of place to place
Across the year each sentence goes
And turning falls to find its grace

Where the line falls no one hears
            and broken phonemes thirst
as if upon ecliptic tears
Where the line falls no one hears
unless she's said out loud or nears
a place of mind to burst
Where the line falls no one hears
            and broken phonemes thirst

                                with Lisa Jarnot

3 *Graces*

108   Amazing Grits! How sweet the Redeye
That flavored my Livermush!
Fried Okra, Collard Greens and Chicken fried
Ice Tea, lots of Lemon with Mint crushed.

Amazing Space! How intergalactic the Wormhole
That beamed up a Quark like me—
I once was Kirk, but now I'm Spock
Was Tribble in another Quantum Reality.

Amazing Grace, I have loved you
Ever since we were in grade 1-B
You wore a tight skirt
To please I wore a pleated one
But we were both hoods then

You are a psychologist I please by not mentioning
My case to you too often,
So please Grace, let's at last go to bed together
Again tonight in Apartment 9-B.

verse 1) by Lee Ann Brown
verse 2) by Lisa Jarnot & Lee Ann Brown
verses 3 & 4) by Bernadette Mayer

sing to the tune of *Amazing Grace*

Velocity City

———————————

Messy girl —
Wear red accessories!

Transisters

for Laynie Browne

Belly

Sisters polished and died for
Bright both form my excited face

Breeders

Deal a hard match case
352 people do a ludic boxstep

Phair Drive

Love songs to girls
    I wish you to write
but we seem to love the ones
who can't set love back
or settle for us somehow
not what they want

I could please you I know
Love what you could be to me
How I could be with you

Polly Harvey

114   Repeat the rub
        raw ambition welcome thing
freer automatique
        zipper gun shuns my
music to interruption
        "or I cld. kill you instead"
burnt to release make me
        beg for some life before
I die crashing, my skill mixed

Remember the rub
        how it buzzes & chafes—
Chaser no straights
        inked out that lovesick
flavor what next headache
        fixes out messed up
music late to see
        how fucked up minus
Anna the Polly I am now

                    Love sick

                    music comforts

South of the Mind

Covered with lotion
I watch
TV

Desperately Seeking

Dear New Jersey math man
 with Texas drawl
Please be at benches
Monday night. I'm back, had a cold.

tenderly kiss me so
I can be near you

as example of
metrics

O You Plural Familiars

Y'all are moving y'alls
legs too much.

8:15 a.m.

"Want some peardrop?"

Definitions at 3:15

Poetry

a condensed form
of food & time

Voice

my speech
babe

Brain

A rain in B

Boat

Toy bot,
a ted debt

Solitude

Sun in a squee-
gee

Modesty

the ruined package

Discourse

talking fancy
without much to
drink

Foolproof Loofah

Lo! I fill prol pills
Poof! I rail pro lolls
Fool! I ill for lips
O Pale! I foil frail profs
Fop! I frill pale roils–
So! I proof oil spills

April Fool's!

Meow Memo

Moon
eggs sold much
on
world market

Maya yams say "ma,"
Eons–
O
Wow

A Suit(e) Address

two words to Jeff

my "little dyke"
sent me this valentine:
I'll be wrapped around your finger

So much depends upon
a red-handed wheelchair
glazed with raincoat water blisters
beside the white-hot chickenpox

Tennos

for Forrest Gander

Tenor:

Offset dander arrests nested dears, O—
Sand or gar-rounded garrets enrage a bear,
        O
Ten tarot readers are rare, dare to
        Rad,
No—
Render a reader or a tresser on snagged dross, O—
Serene Feds ran and sanded on a Dead Fest
        So,
Garnet gangs off goats to ghosts aghast
        For
a tensor Deos tests a rennet fag rag addressed

Dear O,

        A tenner note: dang sonnet's a tenson.

4th Street Diagonal

for Joe Brainard

an amalgam of hearts
or anonymous flowers

a red ribbon worn
by men passing & nodding

If we all looked alike
How would we fall in love?

Red Raincoat Language

for Jim Brodey

Lying in the tub
listening to yr Jimi Hendrix
  bootlegs
      of VooDoo Child a
  sweet
investigator

be generous &
"impolite among iambics"

To Bed

We must to bed
kind to bed
kindly go to bed now
we must go to bed now
Please will you get in the bed
I'm in bed now and want you
with me in the bed now
Where are you oh you're in
bed now if I go to bed
you'll be there too
and that would be
the kindest thing
to the bed now
to bed

To the tune of "Henry Lee"

122   Git down git down my Tommy Ray
and sing all night with me
The very best lodging I can afford
will be fair better today

Cuz I'll come down, make little sounds
and lay on my lazy right arm
For the love that I have in my very left hand
will guide me through the storm

I write to you amidst this plague
of flying starlings as words
Your sublime voice from out the palm trees
has upset all my birds

The cat's got my tongue as I stroke your side
Don't forget to focus them well
With all my love I close this little song
til you're too near to tell

P Rose Dictation

for Hannah Weiner

A P prose diction
A B rose friction
a friction fiction.
Rose prosaicly fixed up
a marriage. Looking for
ward not black not a
lack. Sacked but not perjured.
Purloined but not lettered nor
severed. A Prose
dictation flowed endlessly
dictionally flowering with unknown
margins not prose or poetry. You are not
Steinian as much as
a stone is. P rose its
merry way across the
page. A pause he said.
We know better, inspired
by summer. A
wild writing across the
binding or being surprised
at the bottom of the page
coming so quickly
posing as fiction, a
box of untruths.
Fiction L through P. I also
carried in a box of
"Theory" & "Poetry"

A through K
for P & L today. O
Santa Fe! Communists
misspelled so as to fool
the government. Fe! Feo!
A comm fe san tea &
sandwich conference.
Patience dear. I'm
on vacation this year.
Down donors how much
can you afford to spring?
Free electric light
published on yr
screen. O
typee /type A
backee achee.
Dictatee thinking veil
autobiographee posé
as fiction.   Bilabial
frictatives conjoin to
undermine the mubject
atter of the confessional
letters A–M or L.
P factors without it
prose is into a rose.
Fiction dictionarily
"nears" untruth.
Poetry makes many
To me "naturally"
new ones
instead of kitty cover-ups

for old worn armchairs.
Who cares for
pose fiction. Not
I prefer watching it
in technicolor or
mysteriously slide
into the pool.

Fresh from the field stars
      Fresh from the fields stir
        French from the feel fields
          Fish three rinse rest
           Rise extracts depart from we
             Three graces times pictured ranch
              Diagonal season resists traffic
                Enthusiastic nonsexual pastime
                  What everyone else ignores he collects
                  Filling from the flea market
                   A road repaired and sullied
                     Meant for teething rings stuck on an island
                     A bad letter writer
                       Fronts as a saucy dog on agreement
                        Contracted disease delight trap
                          "Sugar Control 'Ya"
                           A bad town crier
                             Discontinues to dis

     for Bruce Andrews
     after "Möbius"

A Long Sentence Distance

Write the most beautiful sentence in the world and fill
the whole page with its sinuous references to longhand
inquisitive beauty despite always remembering your girl-
hood friend suicided and the world may not give you ev-
erything you ever wanted asking yourself should I grow
up or never be afraid of happiness take risks expect ev-
eryone to find their level or go elsewhere where you ain't
never been my richer friend Antonia ironically ran into
Edmund just after the lecture I used to audit but now
can't find the time mundanely projected multiplying on
the face of the computer clock colored hot essential etc
you got marked personal but I don't remember doing it
all of the little moments we must think of each other si-
multaneously even desire intensely each other but how
do we know you're probably asleep now or I'm crazy to
call why can't I just write you like that better anyhow but
I couldn't stand to part with that valentine since I know
you don't keep anything maybe I could make something
so beautiful you'd change your ways but why should I
worry so about that your beau present body is what I'm
hoping for some trim rub our starter sets together cat
and mouse or even joke with ugly names like chore girl
weezer willie or lily muff muffin peach or even peachfish
despite the fact I always misspell "exercise" want to put a
z in it or switch the *c*'s and *s*'s neurotically not remember-
ing her hands are still so soft at the end of the winter and
growing older then and now we'll find time to dance a

little bit this summer the strawberries and asparagus my
mother ate in Italian squares would surely be on her list
of things to do again at least my grandmother is writing
now maybe I can get my mother started a little earlier I
did get my family to do a sonnet exercise and they wrote
some great stuff but I don't think my father respected or
understood what he had done wept at the bottom of the
page calling you my best friend everyone needs a
confidante maybe even more than a sexual high thought
I'd never say that or is he being distant so I'll just get on
with things and it won't be dangerously low why do I feel
so low I shouldn't be writing now because it'll get all con-
fessional or something all bogged down in domestic
swamp trying to keep myself out of one confusion now I
understand her confusion right there with the feeling I'll
see my mother soon maybe that's what's bringing on this
weepy mood keep going anyhow one long sentence with
no punctuation I spilled I think what good can possibly
come out of this situation I always ask please no more
public screaming but maybe I perversely enjoy being
chased into traffic like that you couldn't eat me up even
if you tried this isn't a list poem it's just a mood you said
so I told you what it really was that was bothering me are
we all alone or aren't we now I regret missing the chance
and worrying about my as yet unrevealed life trying not
to count on favors but go for the real poem or is this the
thong in the sandal that broke and you had to mail it to
me today I saw a young girl on the green who gave me a
jolt like I thought you must feel seeing her why am I so
scared of the future at this time everything usually falls
into place but I always feel I have a lot of time and maybe
now I don't the furthest thing from my mind is just as

important as what I'm doing now in a way so the trick is
somehow to rotate them all spontaneously and call Her
and see what nutty things have been going on after his
death and why she looked so warm and amazing as if
she's been instilled with some kind of amber liquid the
three daffodils facing in opposite directions he must be
tired after all of these demands still no punctuation even
though it's illegal count down day 45 that's enough just
pace yourself stay here awhile and it'll flow as she says
it's April and it's snowing unlike the interior of my gently
lined inorgasmic stomach the gem exquisite got bored
enough to sit down and do some work forever riding in a
van or waiting with Raquel from Puerto Rico who knows
Gladys and Rosanna and things that are messy girls life
my desk spaghetti not really it's very organized my
mother's office her bedroom and scarf drawer which I
could be looking at tomorrow if all goes well so impa-
tient use that there busy signal wish I could see her early
black writing a line drawing three blue towers Gertrude
and Alice deboarding a plane holding little dolls late May
he'll be gone late cure yourself of bad habits like smok-
ing or procrastination try the re-dial every five minutes
in the meantime social hour on the phone not a good
night for being lonely worn out my welcome with most it
feels like a trip to some other country is in order my
convive some music would help or singing no two ways
about what she's bringing now in away far off trick is some-
how somewhere rotating spontaneously and calling the
great mother of us all to hear her lovely syntax describ-
ing interplanetary space and the sick feeling in my stom-
ach when I realize he's dead and I'm still here did he
want me to do anything in particular did he tell her any-

thing at the last moment or did he just gradually let go I didn't stay there was nothing I could do and his mother was there his death and why she looked so warm and amazing as if she'd been instilled with some kind of amber liquid the three daffodils facing in opposite directions he must be tired after all of these demands still no punctuation even clicking irregularly will I remember where everything goes or will it be disaster like after a war looking forward and never running out in wonderland grow up baby girl but still have escaped the hemp crisis open damp second for illustrative learning sequences Bettina expects me to code and then a little something orchestrate my life hurts my hand very clear with her drive up to Passover but my hands killing me it's Allen naked was he in drugs want to call you earlier not going to do basic things want New York is a fantasy Cat named the terms of existence in these deep waters only a little less hostile than the black reaches of interplanetary space Rachel Carson wrote probably the first book of the ecology of the ocean and this quote is about what it's like for the forms of life Max's little league booming sportsman well Max I just don't Sophie with her amazing purple haze every time I look at her from a distance I get surprised into your sister and her lover see things he's never trees tiny dancer Bo Calloway gardens you know what the Everybodies are coming the movement of the bees over oh god bernadette you look beautiful sleepless and eatingless and mourning now I'm reading it's a stupid religious book you may have sudden headaches it's been amazing can't believe it timely surrealistic show can't get myself up out of my bed better to brood mediate or hide

very quiet with the woman who was doing the cooking
and reneged all of the other tables away read one of his
poems about his parents' death he left in tears just one of
the many it's ok you feel weird if it's any comfort to you
can't do anything yesterday I changing the subject know
that from associate hideousness want to avoid it when I
got your also simultaneously not there for her also totally
freaked out he is her thriving and well inside imitating
his symptoms die a second time of laughter lying in bed
not able to move keep thinking the dreams will happen
the ultimate insult of the natural history of the body all
kinds of angry people shouting at me from every direc-
tion shouting Tom says I'm going out to get some fish
and then Philip is there and is saying I want to get fish
also should be kinder to me thought maybe I could get
through the expectation that I won't have to suffer it's
true it would work be really distracted by a foreign coun-
try be less sensitive believe that person I had a dream
flying together over the rooftops of Manhattan never tried
to have the dreams before and yet all this amazing sexual
energy towards people's eyes seemed really bright like
his whenever I came in with Sophia so brilliant looking
the last time Sophia rose up from his bed stared convers-
ing with him in a wonderful way after Gerard died per-
formed only origin meeting Helen 10 or 15 years one of
those avoiders another mother again kept calling and
wanting to know he was nervous and wasn't responsible
for his being his poetry well you're the only person what
was his death sounds like Keats' death with his really bril-
liant his brilliant features swarming more enhanced his
last words actually called up you've been a traitor to me

you acted forgiven me for both my brother and sister are in insane asylums am I three a success probably sometimes more than others playing word games with others am I going to be a good "dier" already in the hospital young my parents I'm a real poet the book itself lots of water none of us behaved properly should've done things being really wrote can't imagine fell asleep learn how to mourn I think absolute nothingness I've found myself unconscionably attractive look at the way he curves we cruised sometimes we would agree even when incredible desires for strangers a possible fuck look at my bed and often go back to it accepted a work of initial is now insidious different names lazy thought every man I've been involved with having created environment accepted would have me you're not married you're not Jewish you're too old you're a woman wanting a surrogate family also simultaneously parenting methods Gerard's death really alone don't know don't care kind of desperate would like to have family with people older than me young man had make huge meals decided he wanted the priesthood his sister would write me these thirty-pages letters the education of a woman you are a part of our family lost it when you heard it did you ever practice forget it in relation to how much energy I think should have a life of her own expects you idolized hang out never got it how we felt about never ever to please them weather older sister at least for looked up rest imitate completely powerful person especially in a generally torture there tree in loco parentis test guest testy tease in help let her alone how does one act you're the mother and younger sister of me rustled up.

A Little Resistance

Resistance Play

All I need is a little resistance
          to come
           to terms

All I need is to read you
And see how our poems differ
          where they intersect

then fill in the blanks
          for a new poem

Small daily
          resistances insist
on
corrosion of conformity

Re sister your self
          as also an act of kindness to the others
          who enjoy you

You who pleasurably
enjoy your register of pleasure you

Cultivate

for Joe Brainard and Kenward Elmslie

Pansy

Showy, invisible
not concerned with cherry pit
Five sepals, four with black, one cherry dot
leaves mutate
Back hook hooded, capped
point thin vein mouth
monk's rigid tuning
to a hard yellow

Peony

140 moist white collapse
     marilyn's red kiss tissue

     soft drop all at table bunching tinged
     range: mauve, magenta, white carnation blue
     collar of ants populate taste parts
     traditionally departing painfully from an idea

Poppy

Oracle eye
over the couch
color of coral slip cove
thistle bomb
pink shear working
prick round the ball we bleed
edge serrated
hairstem
green degrees dying

Paper white

142   tangle out around straight
dry and wet dark
and connection to white
smooth little bulges around
the top peeling back standing
straight out like thirsting
or spiky thirsty
framing a windy feeling
the fragrance coming out at once
nudging the seeds but
with past bunches of
yellow in the middle
earth rhyming or glowing
not believing touch
smooth and lined too
small to smell now

Daybook

for Steven Taylor

So I found an anatomy of aerial bodies:
                    Arms: Azure on a bend O.
The first day back we sleep like athletes as if
                    There's no end in the speaking of bees.

146   If grammar
        is the way
        the mind "works"
        this includes the music
        of syntax.

        Thinking is daily living.
        The surprise of faces,
        Children uptown.

        Her grasping at phrases.
        Scent of her familiar
        Votive blue.

Spelling on face letters
changes the still object.

L-train all light on
Platform 3.
Pink George Washington,
Mosaic Malcolm X.
A ballroom he spoke
holding.

Fast tiptoe into room articulation.
Get sister's vegetable idea of music.
Hazy bike into
higher beginning.

Spelling is a light skill,
counting articulation sensual.
The room's a wreck full of
stimulation.

Invitation to
Basho's warehouse theater.

Expecting human weather, I
write July telephone.

148   Don't deny that
       You are feeling.
       Everybody
       Needs a building.

Alone

Monk he had antiseptic actions odd
to have changed so much,
hope to be not like the rhyme.

Kind day and kind of grey and kindergarten

Mississippi is Goethe's statue.
The allegory of his aloneness
made for good play.

When I finished peaches
I wash a different part of my
Body: observe aurora phonograph.

Like finders plucking at a counterpane,
irrevocably gone. The second difficulty
plus homemade. Woolen

Statue O R I O N to my mother.

Memory explains sublimity and the way we go
Downtown. In the factory are the taking
Hands we wash out of our eyes. Her kids
really willing. Concordance.
A jewel of etymology hair.

If our door grew dim.
Lined with reply, we wanted to
go out but stayed in line.
Kindness was the stick.

A few messages, very brief: Phrase
and table.

"A Bird Flew By
With A Vowel In Its Beak"

It was A, and A says O!
And O says Yes! Taste and see
What vowels have done to me.
My Aunt's spider. Web dress.
Easy living implies you. Even
The blues sings "I."

Etymologies of a kiss. Silent fire.
Also Algiers. Edge of a garment.
Rivermouth. Vocables. Blood of the word.
Grammar lessons its fits and starts.
Snatching chatter blows through the shifts.
Unlike the sacred. Telling. Like it is.

The unoriginal angel. A scratched back.
Willow mirrors deep song. The sound of her.
The middle of her, empty to hold. Everybody
can't be gotten away. Call and response.
Repetio Delecto. A folio in loco.
Notable logos stems euphony.

Simple economics denotes Rimbaud.

Warm and Fragrant Mangos,
Thirty Calla Lilies

for Julie Regan

Windows with warped glass make the sidewalk look like water.
Your blue silk dress lies on the shiny wooden floor.
You are splashing in the bathtub full of stolen flowers and
    eucalyptus.
I am walking out of our two octagonal rooms, up a ladder to the
    roof.
Even with so much immediate gravity, the pleasurable thinking of
    music is folding down out of the wall.
Beyond new rice paper shades, the next door boy is rubbing the
    inside of his window with a piece of cloth.
I'm raising your movie camera to my eye.
You are cutting up raw fish, accumulating paper, asking me to pin
    you down and make you feel how words are placed in the air.

Heavy Earthly Diadems

Compact body heavy from falling
asleep after work.
Cute sun touches the
tops of buildings, something falls.

Magenta dropping blossoms blur,
heat up, while sore Heather sleeps.

A plunging comforter, stained, still comforts.
Open or shut, his body of light.

Our crick stuck duet hit us
with "don't worry," soft.

154 Let's take off all our clothes,
              Honey, and lie down
     with our skins touching in every place possible.

     Don't let anything come between us—
              Even that cotton T-shirt you have on
     seems as thick as the Berlin Wall.

     Let's press our breasts together and french kiss;
              Anything more I can't speak about.
     Too much description ruins everything.

                              after Paulus Silentiarius

A Critical Approach to Love

"only for a certain amount of time are we wanted"

"She'll go anywhere for a kiss and so will I"

An unexpected relationship will turn
into something permanent
my fortune said.   It would be so much more practical
        to marry you . . .
But then what would we do?

A random kiss to concentrate on.
Does it bloom anymore than if left alone?

I need to do laundry.
I need to be alone to write and think I think
then spend all my nickels calling you.

Axis of my Baby

at a constant light of speed
                     stop action disappearing   trajectory of my story

                          How many boundaries tunnel under science
                              then slow
                              assuming it goes where you put your letters

The only thing holding us back is the speed of light
        Rameau is skipping again   Point, circle, circle, circle,
                                                    disappear

              into the box moving faster than the courtyard
      where my eyes are slicing
                  similar triangles

Her hair questions facets up the middle
              of the volume of a sphere, hemisphere and cylinder

Testing duration, linkage of curves, barriers of rotation,
          the demi-monde vs. the companionate marriage

          which function as a matrix:
                  a box of moveable type or womb
                          handwritten across the city's face

    Dying is far more diversified than is commonly imagined
              and has to do with liquids
                          as do the questions of her pleasure

Lake O

Spring like gerunds glowing
signs of pearl like pacing

A bat or bird or book
shaped music aches
to be opened, bare
with rust as you
are playing an
overture
in fever,
a baby night
literature

a gem sprocket.

To order the sonnet
we took
turns breathing light
air.
Trace
minerals curl
in the side pocket.
The rinsed planet
dovetails few
joints, keeping
space even
so.

Pregnant C

158   Subway company,
        a bag full of books.
        and bottles. The poem "Bottle."
        Seeing men as utterly other for once
        (for once). Slipping
        into cat language.
        Lean to another song.

        Crackling static.
        Dropping "things."

        Writing to remind
        umbrellas to open.
        Irascible fetish
        represents a "world."
        Queen of the scene.
        Re-re-reading not
        on my time you don't.

Bodies Can Move This Way

Very fast like a car or waterfall
Absence gap for stored-up music
Evidence for the stolen nonce
Your trick is all to the good

Our planetary hour
takes jumps
Drop it doesn't mean stop

The fixed will fly perpetually
in the blue hour   some light reading

Silk nets are strongest
Morning glories grow best in poor soil
Music maker   Fire tender

Photos   stones
The air sign to burn
Time   your desire   and circumstance

Lyric

160   Snapdragon fear
        cranks the roofgarden
        world around

        Dire type rhythms
        of envelopes office
        difference from ribbons

        Trendy rejection
        of inebriation
        versus daily in your face
        addiction

        Mosaic destruction
        Baby lamb in dream

        Curlicue patterns proliferate:
        The age winds down, y'all

Daylily Excuses

Sonnets in light near vowels redress

Poison up

This side to wall
"I don't know what I mean anymore"

Tapestry clothes
uneven shade
cyclamen by the bed
violet light

the other's pain

barbed clothes
can't shake it

the difference between the two bodies

Canzone Triste

Drooping by a walking change
Even a sad song resolves

A girl voice
Slightly off key
best hesitating

Just get through
it best we can
Gertrude Stein is dead

Another purple twilight
and my friends lie
in their married beds

One burns a pictured cheek
Ruby plus
a purple girl

Poor Sylvia
how can she stand me
in
An artificial paradise
it is Hell to get into

The Lyric Can Snare

every whipped ideal save for
the one just mentioned

Legs flail under cover
waiting for birthday
or border to unravel
its quick hair wreath

Sound's armours teach moving verbal skills
Motor neurons pitch a fevered reach

The lyric still teases
us into a past perfect stirrup

Feed a cold
Starve a fever
You don't feel like earthly either

I'll be ready when you come
Bright red afternoon

Slow Air

164   A clear difference
        Electric arcs
        Charging up summer
                    Her
        translations of a knowing comes & you
                bounce it back
        To replace sleep
        another kind of accident
            Going into warp nine
        Glossolalia
                    as positively
        avoiding straight lines

        "It's 3 o'clock and the
        rain has localized itself."

Planet Stricken

A tool tattoo
free beauty stoner
atones a jean tangle
a rose in the cut

You in the bed
    wedded to warm stories
A common past pet
A blonde piled high
    and going over the hill

What do women want?
A baby between the bath
    and salad
A violent bank?
A hidden pink

The bladed tool
saw a circular rose
itch a little too early

Sill Song

for Beth Brown

When you're gone
is the rented room
other than quiet
for hymn singing?

           Straight music
           nonexistent
           Your playing
           makes living scribble

Quatrains small
as the hall
or long
as the going on

           Of summer
           slips white cotton
           Swinging at Obaa's
           in that old picture

Too late to
call sister
even if zones
time her bed

Rumbling water
colder butter
Two words jump
across a card

Stilted lyrics
Quilt a needle
Not thinking
of weirder dinner

Biddies nibble
in a box
mailed to you
to start a farm

Moving jitters
Present timing
Counted pout
Looser choice

Read it over
reconsider
Nylon sockies
chicken pockies

Rhythms silly
when you think it
Sneezy pretty
Crepe and crush

Discontinuous Autoharp

for Rebby Sharp

Oh how you
Undo me raspberry phosphate
Raptors from the rafters call me
Rhapsody in gumball kazoo

Consonantal harmonies adrift
Lazeeboy rafts Richmondesque
Gape odalisque refigures teething
Mortals at last outlined

The farthest South Jasper can imagine
A gay plum bun, a purplish heard
I want your lyric sheets
Here's the $2.45 plus postage

Falling down on the Job
Quietly elevating babies
Hymn Sings amongst the decay
Racoonbats with rabies

Tar buckets filled with guess what
kind of snake like autochthonic scales
Tectonic plates shift under Chris
My friend and fresh met frisker

Too tiny for words much less
song where does poetry belong
Everywhere or in this little box?

A gentle Rod spoils no child
Sweet fathers I know and mothering
Blue books and Godard girls slighter
Mercies figure in my mouth

Surprising metallic retail Joan
shows up among the unknown
Uncle in grey turt looks spiff
No spliffs but tamales fillet

Bear reads wine and bows for
mercy missed it Jasper says it
Sister then in cat favor
deliberately shies from meaning

Clearly stanzas must stand for
transfers sevens eights or song
I've always been a visitor where's
my absentee ballet?

Quilting is not one of the skills
A longer line might consist of
Catskill association at best Beth
balls the jack and the salty dog rags

No more slavery above the trembling bed
A robin red breast in a cage
While visions of sugar plums dance in our head
Puts all of heaven in a rage

Despite clinging peaches
The South maintains its sticky hold

As that moss dies away
A new Kudzu emerges
In the water this time

Summery

An undone tropic fell too lush
A canyon climb a bird a thrush
A tea before the ending hitch
The sprite from hell said smoke the bitch

I wandered lonely in the midst
of poets conversing not quite kids
and many lovers ex and all
chasing through the water

Fall

As leaf to leave to lavish to laugh
A gape gaffed taped onto dinner mapped
I batter the dough of those who wert
pommeled to structures suturing work

A septet drunk on eating another
forked forgetting a pallid mother
Hence a fruit a bitter bother
Telling truths a ridden scholar

in
Winter

Pity me where the cold north throes
An arm on my cheek a windy pose
In my very bedroom no heat is there
Except when you climb in and dare

to
Spring

Where roses bud and violents bloom
In a circular saw, riding my room
Inscribed on behest   a back anew
Imploding such that she held my view

Oh spring is here and it's only Feb
How it comes to this impatient Reb
She sang invisibly– not this week
Held time enough for us to speak

Crush

for Bernadette Mayer

Crush specific.

Crush complete.
At your feet.
Crush all over.

Ruling the day.
Afraid to say.
Does daddy know?
I move far away.
Sister shrugs.

176   I sleep with two.
One goes up and one rides away.
One stays up all night.
I think with more.
More than two.
Not deciding but enjoying.
Everywhere colliding.
Working and sleeping.
Writing lying down.
Crushed between him and her is nice.
Crush trouble.

3

We are the daughters of enthusiasm.
With tenderness and dancing.
With late night storming.
Excitement sisters.
Where are my excitement sisters.
At work they are all at work.
We want to talk late into the night.
We want to play tenderly with boys also.
To sleep and work on our nonpaying work,
We try to unite our rent power tryst.
It is seldom these days that we meet.

Assiduous angles in a latin position.
We hide in woods to remember
the simultaneous noise of the city,
wearing the ring of the city.

Southern butter.
Did you expect southern butter.
Our rented reality is a problem.

Trillium.
Trillium and lady slipper.
Lady Slipper is married to Jack-in-the-Pulpit.
May Apple is a name to remember.

4

178   The desire of mothers to please others in letters.
The desire of daughters to wrestle fathers not mothers.
The desire of daughters to please mothers and betters.
The desire of daughters to have mothers and fathers.
The desire of mothers-to-be to please brothers and sisters.
My desire to please her daughters and sons.
The desire of others to please letters in mothers.
The tendency of letters to bloom in nettles.

5

Reinvent love.
Can we reinvent love.
Why reinvent love.
Crush as a way of knowing.
Is it the only way of knowing.
It is a good way of knowing.

6

180   She skirts the issues.
Trims the fabric,
describing dresses.
Climbing stairs
arranging papers.
Tent in the street?
No, I need a few stairs.
Place to brush hair
alone or later with you.

In this family we marry for keeps.
Sometimes stuck in southern butter.
More Crisco makes good biscuits.
A detail you pay attention to.
Get off the doors in the back.
Snuff in a can.
Muff is your plan
and you don't mind if I do.
Flexible Lysander is the cat's name.
Gradually becoming friendlier
with heavy petting.

182   I don't want to keep you.
Objection to emotion.
Object of emotion.
Abject in the ocean.
Going with the motion.
Do you second the motion.
Love anti-potion.
Love and devotion.
Obsession can we talk about something else.
Get it out of the system.
It's inherent to the system.
Systemic, we return to it.
Polysemous, multiplicitous, it keeps coming up.
Polyvalent, with many openings.
Anything can be alongside it.
Nouns and verbs.
Noun verbs noun.

9

The grammar of crushing is scary.
Don't be afraid of crushing.
The crush between love and sex.
Wildness in domesticity.
The magazines are so tame.
A magazine of lifting belly.
Pinched and read.
We all must be pinched and read.
Don't think about his objections.
Something in the middle of the day.
It has to be secret.
Lifting belly or thinking.

184   In the crush groove.
       Gertrude was in the crush groove.

       Multiplicitous in form
       I knew we could go on.
       Polymorphously we walk in the park.
       Organic in form like a fern or a city.

       Many times repeating with slight variation.
       How easily we can bruise.

Fearful of confession,
I brave direct address.
Follow the line of the map until
it takes you somewhere.
She is direct and with a rhythm.
It pleases me to see you so pleased.
I have lived with women and men.
This is very fine.

186   How would I say I love him.
He is lying down to music.
We go together and apart.
I am eventually always separate.
He is loved by me and returns that love in his way.
He is loved by men and returns that love in his way.

13

Some Notes:

"Come go with me out to the Field—"
was written in response to the first part of this exercise given to me
by Keith Waldrop:

Rewrite the following in two versions:
        (1) in the style of Emily Dickinson
        (2) in the style of Walt Whitman

The text:
My sweet, let us go and see if the rose, which this morning opened
its crimson robe to the sun, has not lost this evening the folds of its
crimson dress and its color like yours.
Ah! see how in so short a time, my sweet, it has, ah me, shed its
beauties upon the ground! O truly stony-hearted Nature, since
such a flower lasts only from the morning till the evening.
So, if you will heed me, sweet, while your young years bloom in
their freshest newness, gather, gather your youth: as with this
flower, age will wither your beauty.

                               [Ronsard, tr. G. Brereton]

The section title, *Comfit*, was given to me by Hannah Weiner, who
read it on my arm.

"Thang" was written in response to Bernadette Mayer's catalogue
poem, "First Turn to Me."

"August Valentine": This poem takes its form from Edgar Allen
Poe's "A Valentine" in which the name of the beloved is spelled
out throughout the poem as follows: the first letter of the first
line, the second letter of the second line, the third letter of the
third line, and so on.

"Gerard for Unction" was written for poet, Gerard Rizza. It con-
tains references from his most excellent book, *Regard for Junc-
tion* (available from Spectacular Diseases), and poems of John
Keats and Lorine Niedecker.

"Present Beau Robin Blaser" was written on the occasion of Robin Blaser's 70th birthday, during the banquet in Vancouver, B.C.

"So much depends upon" was written in collaboration with members of my Naropa Writing Workshop, "The Gertrude Stein School of Embodied & Disembodied Poetics" July, 1993.

"South of the Mind" refers to Charlottean, W.J. Cash's book *The Mind of the South.*

"Desperately Seeking" source: personals ad, New York Times, Fall 1993.

"Red Raincoat Language" was written during Jim Brodey Memorial, Sunday, December 5, 1993, The Poetry Project at St. Mark's Church.

"A Long Sentence Distance" was composed during a phone conversation with Bernadette Mayer, Spring 1992.

"Slow Air" contains a parenthetical remark by Lyn Hejinian before a lecture at Naropa, in the tent, Summer 1991.

"Inner Crawdad Buzz" is a homophonic translation of the story from Raymond Queneau's *Exercises in Style.*

"3 Graces" was written in response to Ed Sander's call for for new verses for Amazing Grace. Many of these verses were sung at the Poetry Project as "The New Amazing Grace."

In "A Critical Approach to Love" the epigraphs were remembered from a reading by Ann Lauterbach.

There's a lot more to say about these poems so ask me.—Lee Ann Brown

NEW AMERICAN POETRY SERIES (NAP)

For a complete list of our poetry publications
write us at Sun & Moon Press
6026 Wilshire Boulevard
Los Angeles, California 90036